Alaidine Ben Ayed
Sid-Ahmed Selouani
Mustapha Kardouchi

Recherche par le contenu et classification d'images

Alaidine Ben Ayed
Sid-Ahmed Selouani
Mustapha Kardouchi

Recherche par le contenu et classification d'images

application aux images radiologiques et à la
reconnaissance des visages

Presses Académiques Francophones

Impressum / Mentions légales
Bibliografische Information der Deutschen Nationalbibliothek: Die Deutsche
Nationalbibliothek verzeichnet diese Publikation in der Deutschen Nationalbibliografie;
detaillierte bibliografische Daten sind im Internet über http://dnb.d-nb.de abrufbar.
Alle in diesem Buch genannten Marken und Produktnamen unterliegen warenzeichen-,
marken- oder patentrechtlichem Schutz bzw. sind Warenzeichen oder eingetragene
Warenzeichen der jeweiligen Inhaber. Die Wiedergabe von Marken, Produktnamen,
Gebrauchsnamen, Handelsnamen, Warenbezeichnungen u.s.w. in diesem Werk berechtigt
auch ohne besondere Kennzeichnung nicht zu der Annahme, dass solche Namen im Sinne
der Warenzeichen- und Markenschutzgesetzgebung als frei zu betrachten wären und
daher von jedermann benutzt werden dürften.

Information bibliographique publiée par la Deutsche Nationalbibliothek: La Deutsche
Nationalbibliothek inscrit cette publication à la Deutsche Nationalbibliografie; des
données bibliographiques détaillées sont disponibles sur internet à l'adresse http://dnb.d-
nb.de.
Toutes marques et noms de produits mentionnés dans ce livre demeurent sous la
protection des marques, des marques déposées et des brevets, et sont des marques ou des
marques déposées de leurs détenteurs respectifs. L'utilisation des marques, noms de
produits, noms communs, noms commerciaux, descriptions de produits, etc, même sans
qu'ils soient mentionnés de façon particulière dans ce livre ne signifie en aucune façon que
ces noms peuvent être utilisés sans restriction à l'égard de la législation pour la protection
des marques et des marques déposées et pourraient donc être utilisés par quiconque.

Coverbild / Photo de couverture: www.ingimage.com

Verlag / Editeur:
Presses Académiques Francophones
ist ein Imprint der / est une marque déposée de
AV Akademikerverlag GmbH & Co. KG
Heinrich-Böcking-Str. 6-8, 66121 Saarbrücken, Deutschland / Allemagne
Email: info@presses-academiques.com

Herstellung: siehe letzte Seite /
Impression: voir la dernière page
ISBN: 978-3-8381-7576-8

RECHERCHE PAR LE CONTENU ET CLASSIFICATION D'IMAGES :
APPLICATION AUX IMAGES RADIOLOGIQUES ET À LA
RECONNAISSANCE DES VISAGES

THÈSE PRÉSENTÉE À LA FACULTÉ DES ÉTUDES SUPÉRIEURES ET DE
LA RECHERCHE EN VUE DE L'OBTENTION DE LA MAÎTRISE ÈS
SCIENCES EN INFORMATIQUE

ALAIDINE BEN AYED

DÉPARTEMENT D'INFORMATIQUE
FACULTÉ DES SCIENCES
CAMPUS DE MONCTON
UNIVERSITÉ DE MONCTON

MAI 2012

i

REMERCIEMENTS

D'abord, je commence par témoigner mes sincères remerciements et ma profonde reconnaissance aux professeurs Sid-Ahmed Selouani et Mustapha Kardouchi, pour le temps qu'on a partagé ainsi que pour leurs soutiens financiers et moraux.

Mes remerciements s'adressent également à Dr. Éric Hervet, Dr. Guillaume Durand et Dr. Chadia Moghrabi. Je les remercie infiniment pour l'intérêt qu'ils ont apporté à ce travail et les conseils avisés qui m'ont aidé à l'améliorer.

Enfin, ce travail n'aurait pas abouti sans le support financier que j'ai reçu sous forme de subvention accordée par la FINB, sous forme de contrats d'enseignement et de bourses de mérite de l'Université de Moncton.

Alaidine Ben Ayed

LISTE DES TABLEAUX

LISTE DES FIGURES

TABLE DES MATIÈRES

CHAPITRE III

CLASSIFICATION DES IMAGES RADIOLOGIQUES EN UTILISANT LES MODÈLES DE MARKOV CACHÉS ET LES CONTEXTES DE FORMES 30

CHAPITRE IV

SYSTÈME À TROIS ÉTAGES BASÉ SUR L'OUTIL HTK ET LES VISAGES PRINCINPAUX POUR LA RECONNAISSANCE DES VISAGES 42

TABLE OF CONTENTS

RÉSUMÉ

Ce livre est organisé en deux parties distinctes. La première partie porte sur le traitement des images radiologiques médicales et plus particulièrement elle s'intéresse à la recherche par le contenu et à la classification de ces images. La seconde partie se concentre sur la reconnaissance des visages.

En ce qui concerne la recherche des images radiologiques, nous proposons en premier lieu d'améliorer la variante des contextes de formes proposée par Su Yang et al. [8] en projetant les histogrammes dans un espace réduit qui tient en considération les variations les plus importantes. Ensuite, on propose une nouvelle variante du descripteur de forme connue sous le nom des contextes de formes [2] [3] [4] en y introduisant les notions de la logique floue.

En ce qui concerne la classification, on propose d'adapter l'outil de reconnaissance de la parole HTK (*Hidden Markov Model Toolkit*) [23] pour faire la catégorisation des images radiologiques. HTK est une librairie logicielle qui permet de manipuler les modèles de Markov cachés. Notons que ceci demande de prendre en considération l'absence de la composante de temps pour l'image. Cette contrainte est rectifiée si les composantes des vecteurs caractéristiques décrivant chaque image respectent une relation d'ordre bien définie. D'où le choix des contextes de formes comme descripteurs.

Dans la deuxième partie, nous proposons un système de reconnaissance des visages : les signatures des visages sont extraites via une analyse basée sur l'approche des visages propres (*Eigenfaces*) [38]. Ensuite, l'apprentissage se fait par les modèles de Markov cachés. Cette étude a deux apports: le premier est d'adapter HTK pour être utilisé pour la reconnaissance des visages. Le deuxième est de rajouter de l'intelligence artificielle à l'approche des visages propres.

Mots-clés: Contextes de formes, Contextes de formes floues, Transformée de Fourier, Formes propres, visages propres, Modèles de Markov cachés, HTK, Images radiologiques, Reconnaissance des visages.

ABSTRACT

This book contains two parts: the first one deals with medical radiological image processing and it includes three chapters: the first and second ones deal with content-based radiological image retrieval. The third one deals with radiological image classification. The second part includes one chapter dealing with face recognition issue.

In the first part, we propose to improve the rotation invariant shape contexts based on 2D feature space Fourier transform [8] by projecting data onto a lower dimensionality space that highlights the most important variations. This projection reduces execution time. In addition to that, we obtain better recognition rates. Next, we propose a new approach of fuzzy shape contexts. In order to solve the problematic of radiological image classification, we propose to adapt the HTK toolkit [23] which was originally designed for speech recognition research. Note that we should take in consideration the absence of time component when we deal with image processing. This is rectified if components of feature vectors respect a relationship order, that is why we have chosen shape contexts to extract those features.

In the second part, we propose a three stage system for face recognition. First, facial features are extracted via an Eigenfaces based approach [38], then training and test identification are performed by Hidden Markov Models. The system is built on HTK. This study has two advantages: the first one is to adapt the HTK toolkit to deal with face recognition issue. The second one is to improve the Eigenfaces based approach by adding concepts from artificial intelligence.

Key words: Shape contexts, Fuzzy shape contexts, FFT, Eigenshapes, Eigenfaces, HMMs, HTK, Radiological images, Face recognition.

AVANT-PROPOS

« *Without publication, science is dead.* »

Gerard Piel

Ce livre englobe les publications rédigées dans le cadre de mon projet de recherche pour l'obtention du diplôme de Maîtrise ès sciences en informatique. Elle est répartie en deux parties distinctes. La première partie porte sur le traitement des images radiologiques médicales et inclut trois chapitres. Les deux premiers s'intéressent à la recherche d'images radiologiques par le contenu. Tandis que le troisième met l'accent sur la classification de ces images. La seconde partie inclut un chapitre qui se concentre sur la reconnaissance des visages. Les quatre chapitres sont rédigés en anglais qui est la langue des revues ciblées. La thèse comporte également une introduction, un résumé et une conclusion générale tous rédigés en langue française.

Le premier chapitre porte le titre « *Rotation invariant Shape contexts based on 2D fourier transform and Eigenshapes* ». Il aborde la problématique de la recherche d'images par le contenu. Ce travail a été présenté à la conférence internationale « *Imaging and Signal Processing in Health Care and Technology* » (*ISPHT 2012*) qui a eu lieu du 14 au 16 mai 2012 à Baltimore aux États-Unis.

Le deuxième chapitre, intitulé « *Rotation invariant fuzzy shape contexts for efficient radiological image retrieval* », aborde aussi la problématique de la recherche des images par le contenu. Ce travail a été présenté dans la conférence « The *International Conference on Image and Signal Processing* » (*ICISP 2012*) qui a eu lieu du 28 au 30 juin à Agadir au Maroc.

Le troisième chapitre s'intitule « *Radiological image classification using HTK toolkit and shape contexts* ». Comme son nom l'indique, il met l'accent sur la classification des images radiologiques. Ce travail a été présenté à la conférence internationale « *The International Conference on Information Sciences, Signal processing and their applications* » (*ISSPA 2012*) qui a eu lieu du 3 au 5 juillet à Montréal au Canada.

Le quatrième chapitre intitulé « *Three stage system based on HMMs and eigenfaces for face recognition* » propose un système de reconnaissance des visages basé sur l'approche des visages propres et les modèles de Markov cachés. Ce travail va être soumis à la conférence internationale « *IEEE 15th International Workshop on Multimedia Signal Processing (MMSP 2013)* » qui aura lieu du 30 septembre au 2 Octobre 2013 à Pula en Italie.

Le lecteur peut constater que les quatre chapitres présentent des points communs et que chaque chapitre peut être lu indépendamment des autres, cependant il constatera la cohérence des différentes directions de cette recherche dans l'introduction et dans la conclusion de ce mémoire. À noter que les quatre articles correspondant aux quatre chapitres sont reproduits mot à mot tout en respectant les exigences de format imposées par la Faculté des Études Supérieures et de la Recherche.

Durant la première partie de ce travail, j'ai commencé à explorer le domaine du traitement des images en faisant une recherche bibliographique portant sur le traitement des images radiologiques en général. Ensuite, mes lectures ont ciblé les domaines de la recherche des images par le contenu et la classification : Au cours de cette phase j'ai fait un état de l'art des différents descripteurs de formes, les avantages et les inconvénients de chacun. J'ai fait aussi une deuxième recherche bibliographique portant sur le traitement de la parole, notamment sur les documents et les articles portant sur HTK et les modèles de Markov cachés.

Avant de commencer la deuxième partie de ce travail, j'ai fait un état de l'art des techniques et des approches proposées pour la reconnaissance des visages. J'ai étudié les approches images ainsi que les approches par modèles de visage afin de décider quelle méthode utiliser pour extraire les singularités des visages.

Introduction générale

1. Problématique

La vision par ordinateur a suscité l'intérêt de plusieurs chercheurs depuis les années soixante. En fait, les progrès scientifiques ont mené les chercheurs de ce domaine à essayer de construire un modèle artificiel pour la perception visuelle. Ce modèle devant être capable de simuler la vision biologique. C'est un système de traitement de l'information dont l'entrée est un ensemble ou une séquence d'images et la sortie une description de ces images en termes d'objets (classes) et de relations entre eux (similarité). De nos jours, le spectre applicatif de la recherche dans le domaine de la vision par ordinateur est large. Dans ce travail, on s'intéresse à deux sous- domaines applicatifs de la vision par ordinateur : le domaine médical (recherche par le contenu et classification des images radiologiques) et la reconnaissance des visages.

1.1   Problématique liée au traitement des images radiologiques

La santé et le bien-être des individus a fait l'objet de plusieurs recherches en informatique qui visaient à créer de nouvelles techniques de traitement des images médicales. Dans ce travail, on traite deux problématiques: la recherche d'images par le contenu (*content-based image retrieval*) [1] [19] [21] et la classification des images (*image classification*) [20] [22]. La recherche d'images par le contenu consiste à chercher les images les plus ressemblantes à une image requête, alors que la classification des images consiste à identifier la classe à laquelle appartient l'image requête.

La recherche d'images par le contenu ou la classification reposent sur l'extraction de caractéristiques visuelles : ces caractéristiques peuvent décrire les contours, les textures ou la distribution des couleurs, etc.

1.1.1   Problématique liée à la recherche des images par le contenu.

Chaque image dans la base d'images radiologiques a besoin d'être décrite par un ensemble de caractéristiques qui vont être par la suite utilisées pour la recherche d'images les plus similaires à une image requête. Le choix du type du descripteur dépend de la base manipulée: l'utilisation des descripteurs de formes est non justifiée lorsque le but est de traiter des images de nerfs ou des textures où la distribution des couleurs des images est proche d'une image à l'autre.

Dans ce travail, nous avons travaillé avec des images de la base IRMA (*Image Retrieval in Medical Applications*) [44] des images de mains, de têtes, de thorax et de seins. Nous avons opté pour les descripteurs de formes compte tenu du fait que la forme du contour permet de distinguer une classe d'une autre.

Les contextes de formes sont parmi les meilleurs descripteurs de formes utilisés [3] [4] [5]. Le contexte de forme pour un pixel donné est un histogramme à 2D qui représente la distribution de la localisation des autres pixels par rapport à ce pixel dans un espace log polaire. Cet histogramme donne ainsi une description locale de la forme autour de ce pixel.

Les contextes de formes ont été améliorés en appliquant la transformée de Fourier 2D sur les histogrammes pour garantir l'invariance par rapport à la rotation. Les résultats dépendent du nombre des pixels pris du contour. Étant donné que chaque pixel est décrit par un histogramme de forme à deux dimensions, l'approche des contextes de formes devient couteuse en termes d'espace et de temps d'exécution. Dans le premier chapitre nous proposons de projeter les histogrammes représentant les contextes de formes dans un espace réduit qui tient en compte les plus importantes variations entre les différentes formes. Ceci permet d'économiser l'espace mémoire utilisé et le temps d'exécution. Dans le deuxième chapitre nous proposons un nouveau concept de contexte de formes floues. La méthode proposée est plus robuste aux simples déformations qui affectent les contours (les déformations locales).

1.1.2   Problématique liée à la classification.

Dans le troisième chapitre, nous essayons de résoudre la problématique de classification des images radiologiques, c'est-à-dire identifier la classe à laquelle appartient une
image requête. Dans ce contexte plusieurs travaux ont proposé des systèmes de classification basée sur les réseaux de neurones [19] et les SVM (*Support Vector Machine*)
[20][21][22]. Notre objectif est de résoudre la problématique en utilisant modèles de Ma-
kov cachés (MMC ou HMM (*Hidden Markov Models*)) et en utilisant l'outil HTK [23]
qui a été initialement conçu pour le traitement de la parole. De ce fait HTK utilise deux
contraintes essentielles : l'espace et le temps. Cependant, la deuxième composante, le
temps, est absente dans le domaine du traitement des images. Le défi majeur de mon travail fut de rectifier l'absence de cette composante de temps. Ce but fut atteint grâce à
l'utilisation de vecteurs caractéristiques respectant une relation d'ordre. Ces vecteurs caractéristiques utilisent des contextes de formes comme descripteurs.

1.2.   Problématique liée à la reconnaissance des visages

Ces dernières années, plusieurs travaux de recherche se sont intéressés à la reconnaissance des visages [24] [25] [26] [27] [28] [29] [30]. Le but est d'identifier le sujet
auquel correspond une image requête : Ceci demande de décrire chaque visage dans la
base par un vecteur caractéristique représentant sa signature. Dans ce contexte, il y'a
deux catégories d'approches permettant l'extraction des caractéristiques des visages :

- Les approches par modèle de visage qui procèdent à une analyse biométrique des
  images pour déterminer des mesures décrivant la distance entre les yeux, la forme
  du nez ou la taille de la bouche, etc. [31] [32] [33] [34] [35] [36]
- Les approches images qui tendent à compresser l'information en gardant les données les plus importantes pour la reconnaissance des visages Dans ce cas il n'y a

pas de modèles définis a priori, les vecteurs caractéristiques utilisés pour la mesure de la similarité décrivent le visage comme un tout. [37] [38] [39] [40].

2. Objectifs

Lorsque nous avons commencé ce travail, nous avons fixé trois objectifs majeurs : le premier est de proposer un descripteur de forme robuste et rapide qui assure l'invariance par rapport à la translation, à l'échelle, et à la rotation. Nous souhaitions que ce descripteur soit utilisé pour la recherche des images par le contenu pour être appliqué à des images médicales ainsi qu'à d'autres types d'images. Le deuxième objectif était d'adapter HTK, l'outil de traitement de la parole, pour faire la classification des images radiologiques en incorporant les contextes de formes. Finalement, le troisième objectif consistait à adapter HTK pour réaliser un système de reconnaissance des visages en utilisant un descripteur basé sur les « visages propres » (*Eigenfaces*) [38].

CHAPITRE I

Rotation invariant shape contexts based on eigenshapes and Fourier transform for radiological image retrieval

Contextes de formes invariants par rapport à la rotation basés sur la transformée de Fourier et les formes principales pour la recherche des images radiologiques par le contenu

Alaidine Ben Ayed, Mustapha Kardouchi and Sid-Ahmed Selouani

Le texte original de l'article a été publié dans la conférence « *ISPHT'12: the International Conference on Imaging and Signal Processing in Health Care and Technology (sponsored by IEEE Engineering in Medicine and Biology Society)* ».

Abstract

This paper presents a new descriptor based on Shape Contexts, Fourier transform and Eigenshapes for radiological medical image retrieval. First shape context histograms are computed. Then, 2D FFTs are performed on each 2D histogram to achieve rotation invariance. Finally, histograms are projected onto a more representative and lower dimensionality feature space that highlights the most important variations between shapes by computing eigenshapes. Eigenshapes are the more representative features; they are the principal components for radiological images. The proposed approach is translation, scale and rotation invariant, furthermore, retrieving operation is robust and fast due to space dimensionality. Experimental results with classes of the medical IRMA database demonstrate that the proposed approach produces better performance than known Rotation Invariant Shape Contexts based on Feature-space Fourier transformation.

Index Terms: Image retrieval, Shape, Contexts, Fourier transform, Eigenshapes, Radiological images.

I.1 Introduction

Medical image processing has been one of the most fundamental areas of research over the last years [1]. The major goal is to close the gap between informatics and medicine to improve health care. The radiology is considered as the second producer of digital images. So, the growing amount of radiological data underlines the need to create new efficient tools for medical image processing.

Among the fields of medical image processing is image retrieval. The goal is to retrieve the most similar images to a query image used for diagnostic or therapy. Each image in the database is identified through its corresponding signature. Choosing the best descriptor to extract those signatures is a challenge. In the case of radiological images we do not have textures. Also, all images are in grayscale levels whose distributions are very close. So using textures or gray scale information is not sufficient to distinguish between two radiological images. The best way to define signatures is then shape study. There are two approaches: a global one (known as continuous approach) and a structural one (known as non continuous). For the global approach, objects are considered as one unit curve. The structural approach is usually based on points of interest to divide the contour of the object into segments known as primitives [2]. Among the most robust shape descriptors is Shape context [3]. This work improves the rotation invariant shape contexts based on Feature-space Fourier Transformation [8] by projecting shape images onto a more representative and lower dimensionality feature space that highlights the most important variations between shapes. Eigenshapes are the more representative features; they are the principal components for radiological images.

This paper is organized as follows: Section 2 illustrates previous work on shape contexts. The proposed approach is described in Section 3. Experimental results are presented in Section 4. Finally, we conclude this paper in Section 5.

I.2 Previous work

S. Belongie et al. proposed the shape context feature descriptor used for shape matching and object recognition [3] [4] [5]. The main idea is to extract the contour of the object, then to pick up n points. Selected points do not need to be key points such as maxima or minima of curvature. Computing shape context at a given point is performed by taking it as the center of a log polar coordinate system and focusing on the distribution of vectors originating from that point over relative positions. This distribution is a reach description of the shape localized at that point. The use of a log polar coordinate system makes descriptor more sensitive to differences in nearby points. In this paper, a set of 12 equally spaced bins and 5 equally spaced log-radius bins is used to compute shape contexts (Figure I-1).

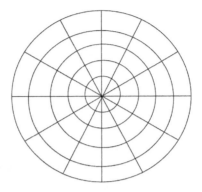

Figure I-1. Log polar grid with 60 bins used to compute shape contexts.

Shape context at a given point p_i is an histogram providing the distribution of the remaining $n - 1$ points over l bins. Mathematically, it is described as follows:

$$h_i(k) = \#\{q \neq p_i : (q - p_i) \in bin(k) | k = 1, 2, \dots, l\} \tag{1}$$

S. Yang et al. proposed a 2D FFT-RISC technique (Rotation invariant shape contexts via FFT) [8]. Computation of this feature is performed by using coordinates and tangents at every point to compute a set of modules and angles $\{(r_{ij}, \alpha_{ij}) | i, j = 1, 2, \dots, n\}$. This set is used to obtain 2D histograms defining shape contexts. Application of a 2D FFT on each 2D histogram provides rotation invariance. The next section proposes an amelioration of the FFT-RISC approach. The main idea is to map data in a lower dimensionality space that keeps only the most relevant information. This makes retrieval procedure more robust. Also, it reduces execution time.

I.3 Rotation invariant Shape Contexts based on 2D FFT and Eigenshapes

For a given binarized image, a reference point is fixed, then, other $n - 1$ equidistant points are picked. Every point is described via its shape context which is a 2D histogram. Each histogram is then reshaped onto 1D vector which is added as a new line to the matrix rehistogram is then reshaped onto 1D vector which is added as a new line to the matrix resenting the signature of that image. The signature is so an M_{nl} matrix where n denotes the number of picked points and l denotes the number of bins. The next two subsections describe the training and retrieval procedures.

I.3.1   Training

A set $S = \{S_1, S_2, ..., S_m\}$ of m training images is used for training. Each image is represented by an M_{nl} matrix which is converted onto a column vector γ_i. γ_i is a vector of z components where $z = n \times l$. Then the average shape vector is computed as follows:

$$\tau = \frac{1}{m} \sum_{i=1}^{m} \gamma_i \qquad (2)$$

Note that each γ_i should be normalized to get rid of redundant information. This is performed by subtracting the mean shape:

$$\theta_i = \gamma_i - \tau \qquad (3)$$

In the next step, the covariance matrix is computed as follows:

$$C = \frac{1}{m} \sum_{n=1}^{m} \theta_n \theta_n^t = AA^t \qquad (4)$$

Where $A = [\theta_1, \theta_2, ..., \theta_m]$ Note that C in (4) is a $z \times z$ matrix and A is a $z \times m$ matrix.

Eigenshapes are the eigenvectors of the covariance matrix. They are obtained by performing a singular value decomposition of A:

$$A = USV^t \qquad (5)$$

Where dimensions of matrix U, S and V are respectively $z \times z$, $z \times m$ and $m \times m$. Also, U and V are orthonormal matrix($UU^t = U^tU = Id_z$ and $VV^t = V^tV = Id_m$). In addition to that:

- Columns of V are eigenvectors of A^tA.

- Columns of U are eigenvectors of AA^t.
- Squares of singular values s_k of S are the eigenvalues λ_k of AA^t and $A^t A$

Note that $m < z$. So eigenvalues k of AA^t are equal to zero when $k > m$ and their associated eigenvectors are not necessary. So matrix U and S can be truncated. So dimensions of U, S and V in (5) become respectively $z \times m, m \times m$ and $m \times m$. Then, eigenshape space is composed by the largest K eigenvectors:

$$\epsilon_k = [U_1, U_2, \dots, U_k] \tag{6}$$

Each projected image onto the Eigenshape space is represented as a linear combination of K eigenshapes:

$$\theta_i^{\text{proj}} = \Sigma_k C_{\theta_i}(k) U_k \tag{7}$$

Where $C_i(k) = U^t \theta_i$ is a vector providing coordinates of the projected image in the Eigenshape space.

I.3.2   Retrieval

Now, given a query image γ, the goal is to retrieve the most similar image to it in the database. First of all, γ is normalized $\theta_q = \gamma - \tau$. Then it is projected on the Eigenshape space:

$$\theta_q^{\text{proj}} = \Sigma_k C_{\theta_q}(k) U_k \tag{8}$$

The distance between the projected image and any other image is defined as follows:

$$d_i\left(\theta_q^{\text{proj}}\right) = \left\| \theta_q^{\text{proj}} - \theta_i^{\text{proj}} \right\| \tag{9}$$

The most similar image is that one corresponding $to\ min(d_i)$.

I.4   Experimental results

I.4.1   Image collection

The radiological IRMA database is used to evaluate the performance of the proposed approach. It contains images of several body parts. Figure I-2 shows some samples of this database.

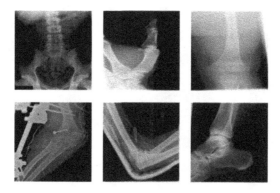

Figure I-2. IRMA samples.

Then, 1000 images belonging to four classes: Hands, Breasts, Chests and Heads are randomly selected. The number of images per class is the same. Figure I-3 shows sample images of these classes. Images in figure I-3 are used in the next sub-section as targets to evaluate the performance of the proposed approach. The Euclidean distance is used to measure the similarity between images.

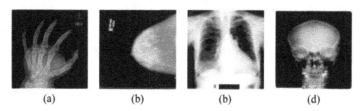

(a)   (b)   (b)   (d)

Figure I-3. Four classes used for performance measurement.

I.4.2   Experiments

Figure I-4 gives an example of image retrieval. Each sample in the top line is taken as a target. Then, 10 most similar images are extracted. The retrieved images are listed in the descending order of similarity from top to down.

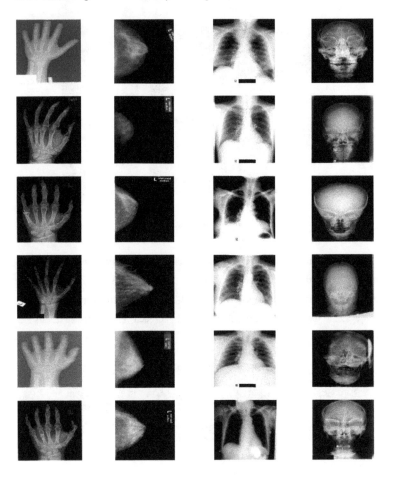

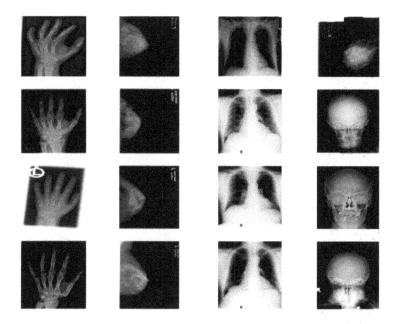

Figure I-4. Example of image retrieval.

To evaluate the proposed approach, recall and precision measurements are used. Precision is defined as the ratio between the number of correctly retrieved images and the total number of images retrieved, while recall is defined as the ratio between the number of correctly retrieved images by search and the total number of samples of the class to which belongs the query image. For each measure of recall precision, the 10, 20, 40, 60, 80, 100, 150, 200 and 250 most similar images are considered. Then, the proposed method (RISC-FFT-EIG) is compared with the FFT-RISC approach.

Figure I-5 plots the recall precision curve for the Hand sample image (a) showing that the RISC-FFT-EIG outperforms significantly the FFT-RISC. Precision rate remains superior to 90 % even when the best 250 retrieved images are considered.

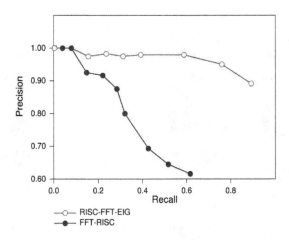

Figure I-5. Recall versus Precision: Hand sample image (a).

Recall and precision curves for the Breast sample image (b) are illustrated in Figure I-6 showing that the precision rate is equal to 100 % for the five first measurements. The proposed approach provides better recognition rates when recall is higher than 0.4.

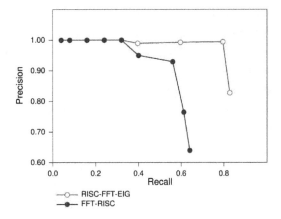

Figure I-6. Recall versus Precision: Breast sample image (b).

Figure I-7 plots recall precision for the Chest image sample (c) showing that the precision rate is 100 % for both of the tested approaches, then, it is higher for the FFT-RISC. However the FFT-RISC-EIG outperforms when recall is higher than 0.5. This means that the proposed approach gives better recognition rates when the number of best retrieved images taken in consideration is high.

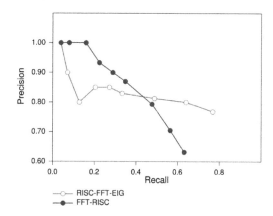

Figure I-7. Recall versus Precision: Lung sample image (c).

To further prove the performance of the proposed approach, average of the precision rate per class considering the best 200 images retrieved is computed. Results are illustrated by Table I-1 showing that the recognition rate with FFT-RISC is equal to 90.72 % while it reaches 95.65 % when the RISC-FFT-EIG method is used. This is due to elimination of noisy data. Another advantage of the proposed method is reduction of execution time which is related to space dimensionality.

Table I-1. Average of precision rate per class considering the best 200 images retrieved.

Image	FFT-RISC	RISC-FFT-EIG
Hands	83.09	98.08
Breasts	85.65	93.47
Chests	98.49	97.01
Heads	95.67	94.06
Average	**90.72**	**95.65**

I.5 Conclusion

Shape contexts have been the subject of several studies due to their simplicity and efficiency. They are translation and scale invariant. Performing a 2D FFT on each 2D shape context histogram provides rotation invariance.

This work has shown that better precision rates are obtained when data is projected in a lower dimensionality space that highlights the most important variations. Furthermore, retrieving operation becomes faster. This is due to the low dimensionality of the new space. Note that the major drawback of shape contexts and their extensions is the fact that they cannot deal with images having many textures.

The proposed approach can be improved by using the Fuzzy logic concepts: the probability of belonging to a given bin is not absolute. So a contour point does not belong to a single bin, however, it also belongs to the surrounding bins with lower belonging probabilities.

Acknowledgment

This work was supported by the New Brunswick Innovation Foundation (NBIF) and the Natural Sciences and Engineering Research council of Canada (NSERC). Authors would like to thank University of Ashen for the IRMA database.

CHAPITRE II

Rotation invariant fuzzy shape contexts based on 2D Fourier transform and eigenshapes for efficient radiological image retrieval

Contextes de formes floues invariants par rapport à la rotation basés sur la transformée de Fourier à 2D et les formes principales pour une recherche par le contenu efficace des images radiologiques

Alaidine Ben Ayed, Mustapha Kardouchi and Sid-Ahmed Selouani

Le texte original de l'article a été publié dans la conference « *ICISP : the International Conference on Image and Signal Processing, 2012* ».

Abstract

This paper proposes a new descriptor for radiological image retrieval. The proposed approach is based on fuzzy shape contexts, Fourier transform and Eigenshapes. First, fuzzy shape context histograms are computed. Then, a 2D FFT is performed on each 2D histogram to achieve rotation invariance. Finally, histograms are projected onto a lower dimensionality feature space whose basis is formed by a set of vectors called Eigenshapes. They highlight the most important variations between shapes. The proposed approach is translation, scale and rotation invariant. Classes of the medical IRMA database are used for experiments. Comparison with the known approach rotation invariant shape contexts based on feature-space Fourier transformation proves that the proposed method is faster, more efficient, and robust to local deformations.

Index Terms: Image retrieval, Fuzzy Shape Contexts, Fourier transform, Eigenshapes, Radiological images.

II.1   Introduction

One of the most vivid fields of computer vision research is medical image processing [1] [10]. Medical image tools are used by physicians for diagnosis. So many works proposed new techniques of medical image processing [11] [12] [13] [14].

Medical image retrieval is a branch of medical image processing. The concept of content based image retrieval is used in many applications such as breast cancer diagnosis systems [15] [16] [19]. Each image in the database needs to be described by features providing its signature. Features extraction is based on visual characteristics. The best features when dealing with simple radiological image retrieval is shape information. In fact, using gray level based approaches is not sufficient. They are in most of cases coupled with edge detection techniques [18]. This work deals with shape descriptors. It improves the rotation invariant shape contexts based on feature-space Fourier transformation [8]. First, fuzzy shape context histograms are computed. Then, a 2D FFT is performed on each 2D histogram. Next, data is projected onto a more representative feature space highlighting the most important variations between shapes. Eigenshapes form the basis of the new space. This will be more detailed in the next section.

This paper is organized as follows: Section 2 presents the proposed approach. Section 3 presents experimental results. The conclusion comes in section 4.

II.2 Rotation invariant fuzzy shape contexts based on Eigenshapes and shape contexts

II.2.1 Previous work

S. Belongie et al. initially proposed the Shape context feature descriptor used for shape matching and object recognition [3] [4] [5]. The proposed approach inspired many authors to propose variants of this descriptor [6] [7]. S. Yang and Y. Wang proposed the rotation invariant shape contexts based on feature-space Fourier transformation [8]. The main idea is to extract the shape of the object and pick up n points. They do not need to be key points such as corners. Shape context at a given point p_i is an histogram providing the distribution of vectors originating from p_i over relative positions by considering p_i as the center of a log polar coordinate system (Figure II-1). This distribution provides a reach description of the shape localized at that point.

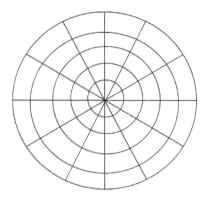

Figure II -1. Log polar grid with 60 bins used to compute shape contexts.

Shape context at a given point p_i is defined as follows:

$$h_i(k) = \#\{ q \neq p : (q - p_i) \text{ bin}(k) \qquad\qquad (1)$$

Indeed, coordinates and tangents at each point are used to compute a set $\{(r_{ij}, \alpha_{ij}) \mid i,j = 1,2,\dots,n\}$ of magnitudes and angles. For a point p_i, magnitudes are obtained by first computing distances l_{ij} between p_i and the remaining points:

$$l_{ij} = \sqrt{(x_j - x_i)^2 + (y_j - y_i)^2} \qquad\qquad (2)$$

Then, a log scale is performed on all distances. Note that length normalization is needed. Thus, every magnitude is divided by the mean distance r_0. Finally r_{ij} is determined as:

$$r_{ij} = \frac{\log(l_{ij})}{r_0} \qquad\qquad \dots(3)$$

Angles α_{ij} are defined as follows:

$$\alpha_{ij} = \arctan\left(\frac{y_j - y_i}{y_j + y_i}\right) \qquad\qquad (4)$$

The obtained set $\{(r_{ij}, \alpha_{ij}) \mid i,j = 1,2,\dots,n\}$ is used to compute the 2D histogram defining the shape context. Application of a 2D FFT on this 2D histogram provides rotation-invariance [8].

II.2.2   Fuzzy shape contexts

The main idea behind fuzzy shape contexts concept consists in considering that the belonging of a contour pixel to a given bin is not absolute. It also belongs to the surrounding bins with smaller weights. This makes the descriptor more robust to local deformations. Figure II-2 shows the case of a local shape deformation supposing that a log-polar grid of four bins is used to compute shape context histograms. A pixel belongs to a given bin with weight $w_1 = 0.7$. It also belongs to the previous and next bins with weights $w_2 = w_3 = 0.15$.

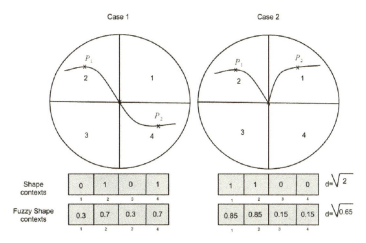

Figure II -2. A comparison between Shape contexts and Fuzzy Shape Contexts (illustration with one level-four bins).

The Euclidean distance is used to measure the similarity between histograms. It equals $\sqrt{2}$ when shape contexts are used. However, equals $\sqrt{0.65}$ when dealing with fuzzy shape contexts which are proven more robust to local deformations. Note that the difference $\delta = \sqrt{2} - \sqrt{0.65}$ is note huge. This is due to the fact that we are dealing with a local deformation. In the rest of this work, a set of 12 equally log bins and 5 equally log radius bins is used to compute fuzzy shape contexts (Figure II-3). Weights of belonging to a given bin are set empirically. There are three cases:

- A given pixel belongs to a bin of level $L1$ with weight $w1 = 0.8$ and belongs to the next and the precedent bins with weight $w_1' = 0.1$ for each (Eg. Bin A).
- A given pixel belongs to a given bin of level L2, L3 or L4 with weight $w_2 = 0.6$ and belongs to all the surrounding bins with weight $w_2' = 0.05$ for each (Eg. Bin B).
- A given pixel belongs to a given bin of level $L5$ with weight $w_3 = 0.75$ and belongs to all the surrounding bins with weight $w_3' = 0.05$ for each (Eg. Bin C).

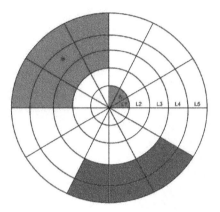

Figure II -3. Weight assignation.

II.2.3 Eigenshapes

For a given image, a reference point corresponding to the closest pixel to the top left image corner is fixed. The next step is to pick up other $n - 1$ equidistant points. Every point is described via its fuzzy shape context which is a 2D histogram. Each histogram is then reshaped onto a 1D vector which is added as a new line to the matrix representing the signature of that image. The signature is so a $n \times l$ matrix where n denotes the number of picked points and l denotes the number of bins. The next two sub-sections describe the training and recognition procedures.

1. Training

A set $S = \{S_1, S_2, ..., S_m\}$ of m images is used for training. Each image is represented by a $n \times l$ matrix. Each matrix is converted onto a column vector γ_l. γ_l is a $z \times 1$ vector where $z = n \times l$. Then, the average shape vector τ is computed as follows:

$$\tau = \frac{1}{m} \sum_{l=1}^{m} \varphi_l \qquad (5)$$

Next, each γ_l is normalized by subtracting the mean shape:

$$\theta_i = \gamma_i - \tau \tag{6}$$

Then, the covariance matrix C is computed as follows:

$$C = \frac{1}{m} \sum_{n=1}^{m} \theta_n \theta_n^t = AA^t \tag{7}$$

Where $A = [\theta_1, \theta_2, ..., \theta_m]$. Note that C in (7) is a $z \times z$ matrix and A is a $z \times m$ matrix. Eigenshapes are the eigenvectors U_l of AA^t.

Note that the matrix AA^t is very large so it is not practical for computations because of its dimension. Also, note that AA^t and A^tA have the same eigenvalues and their eigenvectors are related as follows: $U_l = AV_l$. Next, eigenvectors of A^tA are computed. Finally, m eigenvectors of AA^t are obtained following the relation: $U_l = AV_l$. Only k eigenvectors corresponding to the largest eigenvalues are kept. They form the basis of the new eigenshape space:

$$\epsilon_k = [U_1, U_2, ..., U_k] \tag{8}$$

Each normalized shape in the training database is so projected in the new space. It is represented as a linear combination of k eigenshapes:

$$\theta_i^{proj} = \sum_{j=1}^{k} W_j U_j \tag{9}$$

Where $W_j = U_j^t \theta_i$. Next, every normalized training shape θ_i is represented by a vector ω^i providing its coordinates in the new eigenshape space where:

$$\omega^i = \begin{pmatrix} W_1^i \\ \vdots \\ W_k^i \end{pmatrix} \tag{10}$$

2. Retrieval

Now, given a query image, the goal is to retrieve the most similar image to it in the database. First, it is reshaped onto a column vector σ. Then, it is normalized: $\rho = \sigma - \tau$ .The next step is to project it on the eigenshape space.

$$\rho_q^{proj} = \sum_{i=1}^{k} W_i U_i \tag{11}$$

where $W_i = U^t \rho$. Finally, ρ is represented as:

$$\mu = \begin{pmatrix} W_1 \\ \vdots \\ W_k \end{pmatrix} \tag{12}$$

The last step is to compute $d = \min_l \lVert \mu - \omega^l \rVert$. The corresponding image to vector ω^l is considered as the most similar one to the query image.

II.3 Experiments

II.3.1 Image collection

The radiological IRMA database is used for experiments. It includes images of several body parts. Figure II-4 shows some IRMA database samples.

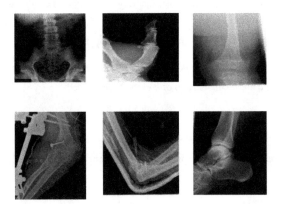

Figure II -4. IRMA samples.

A set of 1000 images belonging to four classes (Hands, Breasts, Chests and Heads) is used. The number of images per class is the same. Figure II-5 shows sample images of these classes.

Figure II -5. Four classes used for performance measurement.

Images in Figure 5 are randomly picked. They are used in the next sub-section as targets to evaluate the performance of the proposed approach. The Euclidean distance is used to measure the similarity between images.

II.3.2 Experimental results

To evaluate the proposed approach, recall and precision measurements are used. Recall is defined as the ratio between the number of correctly retrieved images and the total number of images retrieved while precision is defined as the ratio between the number of correctly retrieved images by search and the total number of images used for test. For each measure of recall precision, the 10, 20, 40, 60, 80, 100, 150, 200 and 250 most similar images are taken in consideration. Figures II-6, II-7 and II-8 plot recall versus precision for three tested approaches:

- FFT-RISC: Rotation-invariant shape contexts based on FFT [8].
- RISC-FFT-EIG: Rotation invariant shape contexts based on Fourier transform and eigenshapes: histograms obtained by FFT-RISC are projected onto a new eigenshape space.
- FUZZY-RISC-FFT-EIG: Fuzzy Rotation invariant shape contexts based on Fourier transform and Eigenshapes: Histograms obtained by FFT-RISC when using fuzzy bins are projected onto a new eigenshape space.

Figure II-6 shows the recall precision curve for the Hand sample image (a) where Fuzzy RISC-FFT-EIG and RISC-FFT-EIG outperform significantly the FFT-RISC approach.

Even when considering the best 250 retrieved images, precision rate remains superior to 90 %.

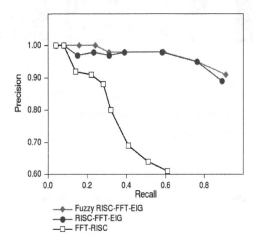

Figure II -6. Recall vs. Precision for the Hand sample (a).

Recall and precision curve for the Breast sample image (b) is illustrated by Figure II-7. The precision rate is equal to 100 % for the first five measurements for all of the three approaches. Fuzzy RISC-FFT-EIG and RISC-FFT-EIG provide better recognition rates than FFT-RISC when recall is higher than 0.4.

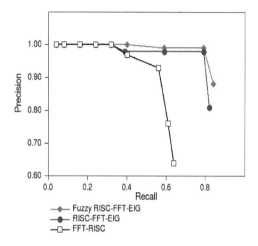

Figure II -7. Recall Vs. Precision for the Breast sample (b).

Figure II-8 shows recall precision curve for the Chest image sample (d). For the first measure, the precision rate is equal to 100 % for all of the tested approaches. Then, it is higher when using FFT-RISC. However the Fuzzy RISC-FFT-EIG and RISC-FFT-EIG outperform when recall is higher than 0.5.

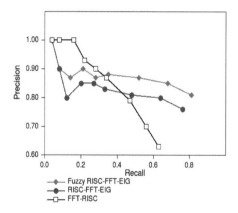

Figure II -8. Recall vs. Precision for the Chest sample (c).

To further prove the performance of the proposed approach, the average of the precision rate per class is computed considering the best 200 images retrieved. Results are illustrated by table II-1 showing that Fuzzy RISC-FFT-EIG and RISC-FFT-EIG outperform the FFT-RISC approach.

Table II-1. Average of the precision rate per class considering the best 200 images retrieved.

Image	FFT-RISC	RISC-FFT-EIG	Fuzzy RISC-FFT-EIG
Hands	83.09	98.08	98.64
Breasts	85.65	93.47	94.1
Chests	98.49	97.01	97.92
Heads	95.67	94.06	94.02
Average	90.72	95.65	96.16

II.3.3   Discussion

Experimental results show that better results are obtained when histograms are projected onto a new eigenshape space. The average of precision rate per class considering the best 200 images retrieved with RISC-FFT-EIG reaches 95.65 % while it is equals 90.72 % with FFT-RISC. Other point to note is that using fuzzy shape contexts ameliorates results. In this case, the recognition rate is 96.16 %. Indeed, fuzzy shape contexts are more robust to local deformations. Note that there is no significant gap between results obtained by RISC-FFT-EIG and Fuzzy RISC-FFT-EIG approaches. In fact, local deformations do not affect significantly the performance of retrieval.

II.4   Conclusion

Shape context has been proven a very powerful shape descriptor. It is translation and scale invariant. Rotation invariance is achieved by application of 2D FFTs on the 2D histograms.

This work proves that using fuzzy bins makes the descriptor more robust to local deformations. Also, projecting data onto a lower dimensionality space highlighting the most important variations between shapes reduces time execution. In addition to that, better recognition rates are obtained. Note that the major limitation of the proposed descriptor is the fact that it cannot be used when dealing with images having many textures.

The proposed approach can be improved if weights are set in respect to the linear distance between each pixel and the surrounding bins.

Acknowledgment

This work was supported by the New Brunswick Innovation Foundation (NBIF) and the Natural Sciences and Engineering Research council of Canada (NSERC). Authors would like to thank University of Ashen for the IRMA database.

CHAPITRE III

RADIOLOGICAL IMAGE CLASSIFICATION USING HMMS AND SHAPE CONTEXTS

CLASSIFICATION DES IMAGES RADIOLOGIQUES EN UTILISANT LES MMCS ET LES CONTEXTES DE FORMES

Alaidine Ben Ayed, Sid-Ahmed Selouani, Mustapha Kardouchi and Yacine Benahmed

Le texte original de l'article a été publié dans la conférence « *ISSPA 2012 : the International Conference on Information Science, Signal processing and their applications* ».

Abstract

This paper presents a new system for radiological image classification. The proposed system is built on Hidden Markov Models (HMMs). In this work, the Hidden Markov Models Toolkit (HTK) is adapted to deal with image classification issue. HTK was primarily designed for speech recognition research. Features are extracted through Shape context descriptor. They are converted to HTK format by first adding headers, then, representing them in successive frames. Each frame is multiplied by a windowing function. Features are used by HTK for training and classification. Classes of the medical IRMA database are used in experiments. A comparison with a neural network based system shows the efficiency of the proposed approach.

Index Terms: Image classification, Shape context, Hidden Markov Models, Radiological images.

III.1 Introduction

Medical image processing has been an extremely active axe of research over the last years. Those researches aim to propose new efficient techniques of medical image processing to improve health care.

Medical image classification is a branch of medical image processing. It is a kind of pattern recognition problem involving two major phases: The first one is feature extraction. The second one is training and recognition test. The first phase is performed by describing each image by its corresponding signature. Signatures are generally extracted through shape study. Indeed, radiological images do not have textures, also, they are in gray scale levels whose distributions are very close. So, using textures or gray scale information is not sufficient to distinguish between two radiological images. In the second phase, extracted features are used for training and test. In this context, previous works on medical image classification proposed classic systems based on neural networks [19] and support vector machines [20] [21] [22].

This paper proposes a new HMM based classifier of radiological images. The system is built on the Hidden Markov Models toolkit [23]. HTK was developed at the Machine Intelligence Laboratory of the Cambridge University Engineering Department. It was originally designed to deal with speech recognition research. Note that in speech recognition procedure, there are two components: time and space. However, in the image processing domain, the first component is absent. This can be rectified if components of feature vectors follow a relationship order. Using Shape contexts based descriptor [3] [4] [5] [8] guarantees this condition. This will be detailed in section 2.

This paper is organized in five sections. Section 2 explains feature extraction procedure. Section 3 describes the new proposed approach. Section 4 illustrates experimental results. Finally, section 5 offers some concluding remarks.

III.2 Feature extraction

III.2.1 Data pre-processing

Images taken from the IRMA database are used in this work. IRMA includes images of many organs such as chests, spines, hands, etc. Sample images belonging to four main classes: Hands, Heads, Lungs and Breasts (Figure III-1) are randomly selected to be used to evaluate the proposed approach.

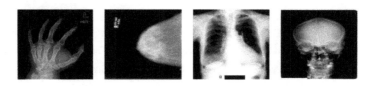

Figure III -1. Samples of images taken from different classes.

III.2.2 Feature extraction

S. Belongie et al. proposed a new shape descriptor for shape matching and content based image retrieval (CBIR) [3]. To obtain shape features, the first step is to extract the contour of the object, then, to pick up n points. Selected points do not need to be key points such as maxima or minima of curvatures. The main idea is to compute shape contexts at every selected point p_i, this is performed by taking it as the centre of a log polar coordinate system. Distribution of vectors originating from that point over relative positions is a reach description of the shape at that point. Note that the use of log polar coordinate system makes the system more sensitive to differences in nearby points. 12 equally spaced bins and 5 equally spaced radius bins are used to compute shape contexts (Figure III-2).

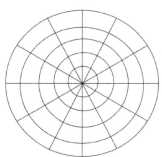

Figure III -2. A grid of 60 Concentric bins.

Shape context at a given point p_i is mathematically defined as follows:

$$h_i(k) = \#\{\, q \neq p_i : (q - p_i) \in bin(k)\,\} \qquad (1)$$

It is an histogram providing the distribution of remaining $n \times 1$ points over K bins. Each image in the database is then described by computing n 2D histograms which are shape contexts corresponding to selected contour points. To achieve rotational invariance needed in the case of breast images (Figure III-3), a 2D FFT is performed on each 2D histogram [8]. Each histogram is then reshaped onto 1D vector and added as a new line to the matrix representing that image. Each image is so described by an $n \times k$ matrix where n denotes the number of computed shape contexts and k denotes the number of bins.

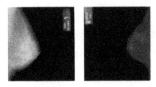

Figure III -3. Samples of breast images where rotation invariance is needed.

III.3 Proposed method

HTK offers many tools for training, testing and result analysis. It is an efficient toolkit that was preliminary used for speech recognition research. In this work, we adapt HTK to deal with image classification: first, signatures are extracted, then, converted to HTK format. Those signatures are injected onto a double stage system for training and recognition test. Training and recognition are respectively performed by Baum-Welch and Viterbi algorithms [23]. The main procedure is detailed in the next three subsections.

III.3.1 Converting features to HTK format

Each image in the database is identified by a matrix representing its signature. Initially those matrixes are saved in a text format. Note that HTK cannot process on those crud formats. Signatures are converted to HTK format. This is performed by representing them as a sequence of samples preceded by a 12 bytes long header containing the following data: a 2-byte integer providing the *number of bytes per sample*, a 4-byte integer providing the *number of samples* in the corresponding HTK file, a 2-byte integer indicating the *sample kind* and a 4-byte integer providing the *sample period* in 100 ns units. *Sample Kind* is generally set as WAVEFORM when dealing with speech recognition. In this case, it is a USER defined *sample kind*. Signature matrix is then converted into a sequence of contiguous samples represented as successive frames. Each frame is then multiplied by a windowing function (Hamming function). This allows a compact representation of their spectral properties. Figure III-4 illustrates header source information of a HTK file corresponding to a Head sample image of the IRMA database.

```
 Sample Bytes:  240        Sample Kind:    USER
 Num Comps:     60         Sample Period:  10000.0 us
 Num Samples:   100        File Format:    HTK
------------------------------------ Samples: 0->3 ------------------------------------
0:       0.000    0.000    0.000    0.000    0.000    0.000    0.000    0.000   21.000   21.000
         0.000    0.000    0.000    0.000    0.000    0.000    2.000    6.000    0.000    0.000
         0.000    7.000    8.000    0.000    0.000    0.000    0.000    0.000    8.000    0.000
         0.000    0.000    0.000    0.000    9.000    0.000    0.000    0.000    0.000    0.000
         4.000    0.000    0.000    0.000    0.000    0.000    5.000    0.000    1.000    0.000
         0.000    0.000    3.000    0.000    0.000    0.000    0.000    1.000    1.000    0.000
1:       0.000    0.000    0.000    0.000   19.000    0.000    0.000   19.000    1.000    0.000
         0.000    0.000    0.000    0.000    0.000   13.000    2.000    0.000    0.000    0.000
        18.000    0.000    0.000    0.000    0.000    0.000    0.000    9.000    0.000    0.000
         0.000    0.000    5.000    0.000    0.000    0.000    0.000    0.000    0.000    3.000
         0.000    0.000    0.000    0.000    0.000    4.000    0.000    0.000    1.000    0.000
         0.000    3.000    0.000    0.000    0.000    0.000    0.000    3.000    0.000    0.000
2:       0.000    0.000    0.000   28.000    3.000    0.000    0.000    6.000    0.000    0.000
         0.000    0.000    0.000    0.000    7.000   10.000    0.000    0.000    0.000   17.000
         0.000    0.000    0.000    0.000    0.000    0.000    8.000    0.000    0.000    0.000
         0.000    9.000    0.000    0.000    0.000    0.000    0.000    0.000    3.000    0.000
         0.000    0.000    0.000    3.000    0.000    0.000    0.000    0.000    1.000    2.000
         0.000    0.000    0.000    0.000    0.000    2.000    1.000    0.000    0.000    0.000
3:       0.000    0.000   25.000   22.000    0.000    0.000    0.000    0.000    0.000    0.000
         0.000    0.000    0.000    8.000    4.000    0.000    0.000    0.000    3.000    5.000
         0.000    0.000    0.000    0.000    0.000    8.000    0.000    0.000    0.000    0.000
         0.000    7.000    0.000    0.000    0.000    0.000    0.000    4.000    0.000    0.000
         0.000    0.000    0.000    4.000    0.000    0.000    0.000    0.000    1.000    4.000
         0.000    0.000    0.000    0.000    0.000    4.000    0.000    0.000    0.000    0.000
------------------------------------------ END ------------------------------------------
```

Figure III -4. A HTK format file.

This work deals with four events. The goal is to determine the class of a query image: to determine if it is a Hand, a Head, a Breast or a Lunge. Each event is defined by a HMM prototype. This requires defining the number of states, the observation function and the transition matrix between states. Figure III-5 shows a sample HMM prototype.

```
<BeginHMM>

     <NumStates> 62 <VecSize> 60 <USER> <nullD> <diagC>
     <StreamInfo> 1 60

     <State> 2 <NumMixes> 1
     <Stream> 1
     <Mixture> 1 1.0

          <Mean> 60
          0.0 0.0 0.0 0.0 0.0 0.0 0.0 0.0 0.0 0.0 0.0 0.0 0.0 0.0 0.0 0.0 0.0 0.0  ... 0.0
          <Variance> 60
          1.0 1.0 1.0 1.0 1.0 1.0 1.0 1.0 1.0 1.0 1.0 1.0 1.0 1.0 1.0 1.0  ... 1.0

     <State> 3 <NumMixes> 1
                                        (.....)

     <State> 61 <NumMixes> 1
     <Stream> 1
     <Mixture> 1 1.0

          <Mean> 60
          0.0 0.0 0.0 0.0 0.0 0.0 0.0 0.0 0.0 0.0 0.0 0.0 0.0 0.0 0.0 0.0 0.0 0.0  ... 0.0
          <Variance> 60
          1.0 1.0 1.0 1.0 1.0 1.0 1.0 1.0 1.0 1.0 1.0 1.0 1.0 1.0 1.0 1.0  ... 1.0

     <TransP> 62


          0.000e+0   1.000e+0   0.000e+0   0.000e+0   0.000e+0  .....   0.000e+0
          0.300e-0   0.400e-0   0.300e-0   0.000e+0   0.000e+0           0.000e+0
          0.000e+0   0.300e-0   0.400e-0   0.300e-0   0.000e+0           0.000e+0
             :          :          :          :          :                 :
             :          :          :          :          :                 :
          0.000e+0   0.000e+0   0.000e+0   0.000e+0   0.000e+0           0.000e+0

<EndHMM>
```

Figure III -5. A HMM prototype.

<state> i is a description of single Gaussian observation. It defines observation function of state i. *<variance>* i and *<mean>* i should respect the dimension observation space. The first one provides the variance vector of the observation function. The second one provides the mean vector. *Transp* gives the transition matrix where each value denotes the probability of transition from a state to another one.

Conception of HMM prototypes is based on the chosen topology shown in Figure III-6: In this work we suppose that we have 62 states. State 1 and state 62 are non emitting states. For the remaining states, we consider that each one represents a bin. The probability of staying in the same sate is 0.4 and the probability of moving to the next or the precedent state is equal to 0.3.

Figure III -6. System topology.

Before starting the training and the recognition procedures, the grammar is defined according to some accurate rules (Figure III-7). It is then compiled to obtain the system network.

$phn = Class1 |Class2 |Class3 |Class4 ; (<$phn>)

Figure II-6. Used grammar.

Class1 in figure III-7 denotes the class of Hands, Class2 denotes the class of Heads, Class3 represents the class of Breasts and Class4 is relative to the class of Lungs. The next step is to define the dictionary that provides the correspondence between variables of the grammar and HMM prototypes defined previously (Figure III-8).

Class1	**Hand**
Class2	**Head**
Class3	**Breast**
Class4	**Lung**

Figure III-8. Used Dictionary.

Finally, the recognizer is composed by the network, the dictionary and the HMM prototypes (Figure III-9).

Recognizer = Network + Dictionary + HMMs

Figure III-9. HTK Reconizer.

III.3.2 Training phase

A good initialization of HMM prototype parameters (transition matrix, mean and variance vectors) is necessary to ensure a rapid convergence of the system. Initially mean vectors are set to 0.0, variance vectors to 1.0. Transition matrix is set in respect to system topology defined in Figure III-6. Those parameters change during the training procedure. They are re-estimated following the Baum-Welch algorithm [23].

III.3.3 Recognition phase

Given a query image, its signature is obtained by shape context descriptor and transformed into HTK format. It is then decoded by the Viterbi algorithm [23]. The recognition procedure requires a clear definition of the network, the dictionary and the HMM prototypes. HMM prototypes used in the recognition step are those obtained at the end of n iterations of parameters re-estimation during the training step to achieve the convergence of the system.

III.4 Experiments

The chosen number of states is justified by computing the success rate when varying this parameter. Obtained results are described by table III-1 showing that best results (best recognition rate and lower computations) are obtained when the number of states equals 62. The system does not converge when the number of states is over 102.

Table III-1. Recognition rate for different configurations.

NB of states	16	32	48	62	78	94	102
Recognition %	33.5	99.5	99.75	100	100	99.75	NON

Table III-2 shows the confusion matrix when 600 images are used for training and 400 for testing. It shows that all images are well classified. So the success rate is equal to 100%.

Table III-2. Confusion matrix.

↓True classes	Hands	Heads	Breasts	Lungs
Hands	**100**	0	0	0
Heads	0	**100**	0	0
Breasts	0	0	**100**	0
Lungs	0	0	0	**100**

To evaluate the proposed approach, HMMs based classifier is compared to a feed forward neural network based system by using the same features. Figure III-10 shows success rates when varying the number of epochs where: the proposed system converges at the end of the third cycle. While the feed forward neural based system converges at the end of the fifteenth cycle. So the proposed approach is faster and gives better recognition rates.

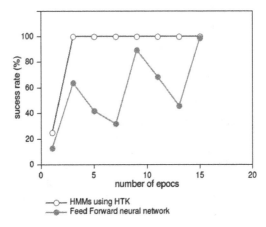

Figure III-9. Success Rate Versus number of epochs.

To furthermore prove the efficiency of the proposed approach, recognition rates are computed when dealing with various configurations (different sizes of testing and training corpus). Results are shown in Table III-3.

Table III-3. Recognition rate for different configurations.

Training	Test	HTK-HMMs	FF-NEUR-NET
800	200	100 %	96.9 %
600	400	100 %	74.8 %
500	500	99.80 %	74.6 %
400	600	99.64 %	71.3 %

When the size of the training corpus is four times greater than the size of the test corpus, the recognition rate is high. It is equal to 100% for the HMM-HTK system and 96.9 % for the neural network based system. When 40 % of the images are used for training and 60%for test, recognition rate for the proposed system remains high. It is equal to 99.64% while it decreases to 71.3% for the feed forward neural system.

III.5 Conclusion

Obtained results show that HTK is a very powerful tool. It can be used in image processing. The use of Shape contexts as a shape descriptor is a good choice. However, several descriptors can be used. Note that components of feature vectors must follow an order relation. This relation enables to rectify the absence of time component.

The proposed approach can be improved by using the fuzzy logic concepts in the feature extraction step: for a given contour point, the probability of belonging to a given bin is not absolute. So, it does not belong to a single bin, however, it also belongs to the surrounding bins with lower belonging probabilities. One other interesting direction for future work is to combine several feature descriptors and use them as inputs to the HTK classifier.

ACKNOWLEDGMENT

This work was supported by the New Brunswick Innovation Foundation (NBIF). Authors would like to thank University of Ashen for the IRMA database and the Cambridge University for the HTK toolkit

CHAPITRE IV

THREE STAGE SYSTEM BASED ON HTK TOOLKIT AND EIGENFACES FOR FACE RECOGNITION

SYSTÈME À TROIS NIVEAUX BASÉ SUR L'OUTIL HTK ET LES VISAGES PRINCIPAUX POUR LA RECONNAISSANCE DES VISAGES

Alaidine Ben Ayed, Sid-Ahmed Selouani, Mustapha Kardouchi and Yacine Benahmed

Le texte original de l'article va être soumis à la conférence « *IEEE 15th International Workshop on Multimedia Signal Processing (MMSP 2013)* » qui aura lieu du 30 septembre au 2 Octobre 2013 à Pula en Italie.

Abstract

This paper presents a triple stage system for face recognition. Faces are initially projected onto a lower dimensionality space that keeps only the most relevant information. Components of this space are known as Eigenfaces. Each face is described via a feature vector providing its coordinates in the new Eigenspace. Then, facial feature vectors are used for training and recognition test by using the HTK toolkit (Hidden Markov Models Toolkit). Note that HTK was preliminary designed to be used in speech recognition researches. Experiments with the ORL face database show the efficiency of the proposed approach.

Index Terms: Face recognition, Eigenfaces, Hidden Markov Models. HTK.

IV.1 Introduction

Face recognition has become a major research area in the last few years because of the need to identify the subject to whom corresponds a query face in different applications. Examples of those applications are security access control, human-computer communication, etc.

Many face recognition methods have been proposed. In this context, there are two broad classes of approaches to extract facial features. They are called constituent-and-face based approaches [24] [25] [26] [27] [28] [29] [30].

Constituent based approaches perform a biometric analyze on faces by computing some measurements such as the distance between the eyes or the length of the nose or the size of the mouth, etc. Some researches proposed eye detection based approaches [31] [32] and their variants such as the concept of eye corners [33]. Other researches proposed to use Gabor filters to extract facial features [34] or chrominance information to locate those features then perform classification [35] [36].

Face-based approaches attempt to normalize a gallery of face images and compress the face data by only keeping the most important information that is useful for facial recognition. In this case there is no prior defined model. Facial features used for similarity measurements describe the face as a whole: [37] proposed to represent faces as a linear combination of weighted eigenvectors by using Karhunen-Loève transform. While [38], [39], and [40] proposed a PCA based facial recognition approach.

To be decoded, facial features are injected in a convolutional neural-network [41] or simply by using a template matching schema [42] or an elastic bunch graph matching [43].

In this work, facial features are extracted by using the eigenfaces based method which is a face-based approach. Those features are used for training and test identification using the HTK toolkit which enables the use of Hidden Markov Models [23]. Note that HTK was designed at the Cambridge University Labs to be used in speech recognition researches. This work proposes to adapt it to face recognition issue.

This paper is organized as follows: the second paragraph describes the proposed system. The third one illustrates the experimental results. Finally, the fourth one offers some concluding remarks.

IV.2 The proposed system

The proposed system is composed of three steps: the first one is feature extraction: Features are initially extracted using Eigenfaces analysis, and then converted to HTK format. The second step is training, which is performed by following the Baum-Welch algorithm, and the final step is face identification by the Viterbi algorithm (Figure IV-1). This will be more detailed in the next three sub-sections.

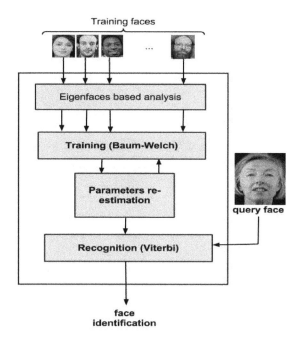

Figure IV-1. The proposed system.

IV.2.1 Feature vectors extraction and system configuration

A. Feature vectors extraction

Feature vectors are obtained via Eigenfaces analysis: each face image is considered as a vector in R^n where n denotes the number of pixels. Extracting feature vectors is based on PCA (principal component analysis). Giving a set of m images $I = \{I_1, I_2, \dots, I_m\}$ each image is reshaped onto a 1D vector. Then, the main idea is to modelize the difference between a query face I_i and a mean face relatively to a set of limit faces called Eigenfaces.

$$I_i = I_{avg} + \sum_h (C(h)U_h) + \varepsilon \qquad (1)$$

So, each face is considered as the sum of a mean face with an average face with a linear combination of Eigenfaces (Figure IV-2).

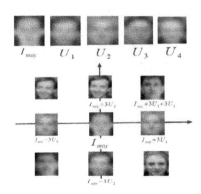

Figure IV-2. Sample image projection in the Eigenfaces system.

I_{avg} is computed as follows:

$$I_{avg} = \frac{1}{m} \Sigma_i I_i \qquad (2)$$

Eigenfaces are the eigenvectors of the covariance matrix AA^t where $A = [I_1, I_2, ..., I_m]$. They are the principal components of face images. Eigenfaces are obtained by performing a singular decomposition of the $n \times m$ matrix A. Then, only K eigenvectors corresponding to the largest eigenvalues are kept to form a new eigenspace $\therefore_K = [U_1, U_2, ..., U_K]$. Each image J is projected onto this new eigenspace as follows:

$$J^{proj} = I_{avg} + \Sigma_k C_J(k) U_k \qquad (3)$$

Its coordinates in the corresponding new space are:

$$C_J(k) = U_k^t (t - I_{avg}) \qquad (4)$$

In the rest of this work, each image is described by its coordinates in the new eigenspace.

B. Features conversion to HTK format

Before starting training, feature vectors are converted to HTK format. This is performed by adding a 12 bytes long header containing the following information:

- The number of bytes by samples (2 bytes integer).
- The number of samples (4 bytes integer).
- The sample Kind (2 bytes integer).
- The sample period in 100 ns units (4 bytes integer).

Then, feature vectors are converted into contiguous samples to form successive frames. To have a compact representation of their spectral properties, each frame is multiplied by the Hamming function (a windowing function). Figure IV-3 illustrates header source information of a HTK file corresponding to a face feature vector.

```
------------------------------ Source: Face 037.htk ------------------------------
  Sample Bytes:  40       Sample Kind:    USER
  Num Comps:     10       Sample Period:  10000.0 us
  Num Samples:   40       File Format:    HTK
---------------------------------- Samples: 0->25 --------------------------------
0:      0.000  -1.000   2.000   0.000  -1.000  -2.000  -1.000  -2.000   3.000  -2.000
1:     -1.000   2.000   3.000  -1.000   0.000   1.000   0.000  -2.000   1.000  -4.000
2:     -3.000  -1.000  -6.000  -0.000   2.000  -2.000  -1.000  -2.000   6.000   4.000
3:      4.000  -3.000   5.000   3.000  -0.000   4.000   7.000   2.000   4.000  -0.000
4:      4.000   1.000   4.000  -1.000   6.000  -6.000  -1.000  -4.000   1.000   4.000
5:     -0.000  -1.000  -3.000   3.000   3.000   5.000   6.000   1.000   2.000   5.000
6:    -10.000   4.000   9.000   1.000  -5.000  -2.000   2.000  -9.000   8.000 -12.000
7:     -6.000  -3.000  -3.000  -4.000   3.000  -1.000  -1.000   6.000   3.000   1.000
8:      5.000  -6.000 -13.000  -3.000  -8.000  -2.000   3.000  10.000 -16.000   4.000
9:      1.000  -6.000  12.000 -11.000  -7.000 -11.000   7.000   0.000   0.000  -4.000
10:    15.000   4.000  -1.000  -1.000   7.000   6.000 -10.000  12.000  -7.000  -0.000
```

Figure IV-3. Sample face feature vector in HTK format.

C. System configuration

In this step, it is necessary to define the HMM prototypes, the system grammar and the system dictionary. HTK is based on HMMs which are probabilistic models. Each group of faces belonging to the same person is represented by a HMM prototype which provides the number of states, the definition of the observation function and the transition matrix. Figure IV-4 shows a HMM prototype sample.

```
<StreamInfo> 1 10
<VecSize> 10 <nullD> <USER> <diagC>
~h "Face__037"
<BeginHMM>

    <NumStates> 42
    <State> 2
    <Stream> 1
    <Mixture> 1 1.0

        <Mean> 10
        0.0     0.0     0.0     0.0     0.0     ...     0.0
        <Variance> 10
        1.0     1.0     1.0     1.0     1.0     ...     1.0

    <State> 3
        .
        .
        .
    <State> 41
    <Stream> 1
    <Mixture> 1 1.0

        <Mean> 10
        0.0     0.0     0.0     0.0     0.0     ...     0.0
        <Variance> 10
        1.0     1.0     1.0     1.0     1.0     ...     1.0

    <TransP> 42
    0.000e+0  1.000e+0  0.000e+0  0.000e+0  0.000e+0  .....  0.000e+0
    0.300e-0  0.400e-0  0.300e-0  0.000e+0  0.000e+0         0.000e+0
    0.000e+0  0.400e-0  0.300e-0  0.400e-0  0.000e+0         0.000e+0
      :         :         :         :         :              :
      :         :         :         :         :              :
    0.000e+0  0.000e+0  0.000e+0  0.000e+0  0.000e+0  0.000e+0

<EndHMM>
```

Figure IV-4. A HMM prototype sample.

<state>i defines the observation function of state *i*, it is a description of a single Gaussian observation. *<variance>i* provides the variance vector of the observation function, while *<mean>i* provides its mean vector. *Tranp* is the transition matrix where each value denotes the probability of transition from a state to another one.

In addition to HMM prototypes, it is necessary to define the system grammar according to accurate rules. The grammar is then compiled to obtain the system network. Figure IV-5 illustrates an example of a grammar in a system classifying faces of five different subjects.

$phn = Face1 |Face2 |Face3 |Face4 |Face5 ; (<$phn>)

Figure IV-5. System Grammar.

The last step to set up the system is to define the dictionary which is a simple text file providing the correspondence between variables of the grammar and the HMM proto-types previously defined. Finally the face recognizer is a combination of the network, the dictionary and the HMM prototypes (Figure IV-6).

Recognizer = HMMs + Network + Dictionary

Figure IV-6. System recognizer.

IV.2.2 Training phase

During the training phase, the parameters of the HMM prototypes are re-estimated following the Baum Welch algorithm [23]. The components of the mean vectors are in-itially set to 0.0, the components of variance vector to 1.0 (Figure IV-7).

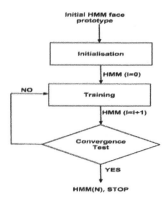

Figure IV-7. The general training process.

IV.2.3 Face identification phase

Now given a query face, the first step is to extract its feature vector via eigenfaces analysis. This feature vector is converted into HTK format, then injected in the system to be decoded by the Viterbi algorithm [23] (Figure IV-8).

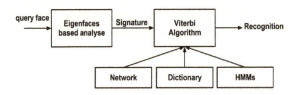

Figure IV-8. The general recognition process.

IV.3 Experiments

IV.3.1 Data collection

The ORL (Olivetti Research Laboratory) database [45] is used to measure the performance of the proposed approach. It includes face images of 40 distinct subjects (10 different images for each) . All the images are taken in up-right, frontal position. Also, they are taken at different times and different conditions by varying lighting, slightly, facial expressions (smiling or non-smiling, open or closed eyes) and facial details (glasses or no-glasses). Figure IV-9 shows some samples corresponding to one subject.

| normal | Happy | Wink | Surprised | sleepy |

Figure IV-9. ORL face database samples.

In the rest of this work, seven images from each class are used for training and the three remaining ones are used for test identification.

IV.3.2 Experimental results

The chosen number of states when defining the system topology is set heuristically to 42 states, supposing that each group of face images belonging to the same person is represented by one state. States 1 and 42 are non emitting states (Figure IV-10).

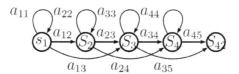

Figure IV-10. System topology.

To see whether it was the best system topology or not, recognition rates are computed using different system topologies. They differ by the number of states. Results are illustrated in table IV-1 showing that the best recognition rates are obtained when the number of states equals 35.

Table IV-1. Recognition rate for different configurations.

NB of states	14	21	28	35	42	49	56
Recognition %	77.5	85.33	86.17	89.17	81.67	NONE	NONE

To see whether the system converges quickly or not, recognition rates given at different epochs are illustrated in Figure IV-11 showing that the system converges at the end of the third epoch.

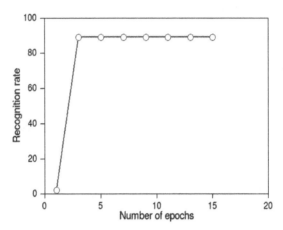

Figure IV-11. Recognition Rate Versus the number of training epochs.

Table IV-2 shows obtained results and confusions made by the system. Note that the global recognition rate reaches 89.17%.

Table IV-2. Obtained results and confusions made by the system

Face class	Confusion(s) with	Recognition Rate (%)
	NONE	100
		66.7
	NONE	100

NONE 100

0

NONE 100

NONE 100

NONE 100

NONE 100

33.3

NONE 100

NONE 100

NONE   100

NONE   100

66.7

NONE   100

NONE   100

66.7

66.7

NONE   100

NONE   100

NONE 100

NONE 100

NONE 100

NONE 100

NONE 100

NONE 100

33.3

66.7

NONE 100

NONE 100

NONE 100

NONE 100

NONE 100

NONE 100

NONE 100

NONE 100

NONE 100

NONE 100

66.7

Total: **89.17**

The recognition rate per class equals 100% in the majority of cases. It decreases in other cases when the face image is very similar to those belonging to another subject.

IV.4 Conclusion

This paper proposes a three stage system to perform face identification. First, facial features are extracted by eigenfaces analysis. Extracted features are used for training and test identification. Also, this paper explains the way to adapt the well known HTK toolkit to deal with face recognition issue. HTK is originally used for speech recognition research, and is based on Hidden Markov Models.

A standard database of the Olivetti Research Laboratory (ORL) including 400 images of 40 distinct subjects is used to evaluate the proposed system. The recognition rate equals 89.17%.

The proposed system has the following advantages:

- It does not require detecting any biometric features such as describing eyes, mouth or nose, etc.
- It converges quickly: only three epochs of training are needed to achieve system convergence.
- It is flexible: the proposed system can be used with any facial feature extractor.

The future improvement of this project will continue on comparing the obtained results when using different facial feature extractors.

Conclusion générale

Les travaux de recherche présentés dans cette thèse s'inscrivent dans le contexte du traitement des images radiologiques (la recherche des images par le contenu et la classification) et la biométrie (la reconnaissance des visages). Nous avons tout d'abord amélioré les contextes de formes [3] [4] [5] [8] avant de proposer une nouvelle approche des contextes de formes floues. Aussi, on a proposé un système de classification des images radiologiques en adaptant un outil de traitement de la parole pour résoudre la problématique. Le même outil a été aussi adapté pour concevoir un système de reconnaissance des visages basé sur les modèles de Markov cachés et les visages propres.

Nous avons commencé notre travail en faisant un état de l'art des descripteurs qui peuvent être utilisés dans le cas des images radiologiques. Vu la base manipulée, notre étude était plus concentrée sur les descripteurs de formes. Pour la deuxième partie de ce travail, nous avons fait une recherche qui a porté sur le domaine du traitement de la parole en utilisant l'outil HTK [23].

La première étude a permis d'améliorer les contextes de formes en termes de temps d'exécution en projetant les histogrammes représentant les contextes de formes dans un espace réduit. Ceci a pour effet d'accélérer la recherche par diminution de l'espace de recherche (section I.3). En outre, le nouvel espace formé est plus expressif puisqu'il prend en considération les variations les plus importantes entre les formes. Ceci est un second avantage pour une recherche plus rapide.

La deuxième étude propose un nouveau concept de contextes de formes floues. L'idée principale est que l'appartenance d'un pixel de contour à un bin donné n'est pas absolue. Car ce dernier appartient aussi aux bins qui l'entourent mais avec des degrés d'appartenance inférieurs (section II.2.2). L'approche proposée est plus robuste aux déformations locales.

La troisième étude a permis de proposer un système de classification des images radiologiques. Les vecteurs caractéristiques sont initialement extraits via les contextes de formes. Ensuite, l'apprentissage se fait par les modèles de Markov cachés. Dans ce travail on a adapté l'outil de traitement de la parole HTK qui permet de manipuler les modèles de Markov cachés. Le classificateur repose sur l'hypothèse que les composantes des vecteurs caractéristiques respectent une notion d'ordre bien définie afin de compenser l'absence de la composante temps dans une image. Le système proposé, comparé à un système basé sur les réseaux de neurones, a montré son efficacité en termes de taux de reconnaissance et de temps nécessaire pour converger.

La quatrième étude propose une méthode de reconnaissance des visages où les vecteurs caractéristiques sont extraits en se basant sur l'approche des visages propres (*Eigenfaces*) [38]. L'entraînement du système repose sur les modèles de Markov cachés. Dans ce travail aussi, nous avons utilisé l'outil HTK. L'apport de notre travail est double. Tout d'abord l'amélioration de la méthode des visages propres par l'intelligence artificielle, mais aussi l'adaptation de HTK pour la reconnaissance des visages.

BIBLIOGRAPHIE

[1] C. B. Akgl, D. L. Rubin, S. Napel, C. F. Beaulieu, H. Greenspan and B. Acar1, Content-based image retrieval in radiology: current status and future directions, J. Digit Imaging, Volume 24, pp. 208-222, 2011.

[2] D. Zhang and G. Lu', Review of shape representation and description techniques, J. Pattern Recognition, Volume 37, pp. 1-19, 2004.

[3] S. Belongie and J. Malik, Matching with Shape Contexts, IEEE Workshop on Content-based access of Image and Video-Libraries, 2000.

[4] S. Belongie, J. Malik and J. Puzicha, Shape Context: A new descriptor for shape matching and object recognition, In NIPS, pp. 831-837, 2001.

[5] S. Belongie, J. Malik and J. puzicha, Shape Matching and Object Recognition Using Shape Contexts, J. Pattern Analysis and Machine Intelligence, IEE transaction, Volume 24, pp. 509 - 522, 2002.

[6] A. Diplaros, T. Gevers and I. Patras, Color-Shape Context for Object Recognition, IEEE Workshop on Color and Photometric Methods in Computer Vision, in conjunction with the 9th Int. Conf. J. Computer Vision, 2004.

[7] M. Kortgen, G-J Park, M. Novotni and R. Klein, 3D Shape Matching with 3D Shape Contexts.

[8] S. Yang and Y. Wang, Rotation Invariant Shape Contexts based on Feature-space Fourier Transformation, Image and Graphics (ICIG), Fourth International conference, pp. 575-579, 2007.

[9] M. Turk and A. Pentland, Eingenfaces for recognition, Cognitive Neuroscience, Volume 19, pp. 71-96, 1991.

[10]   H. Muller, N. Michoux, D. Bandon and A. Geissbuhler, A review of Content-based image retrieval systems in medical applications-clinical benefits and future directions, International Journal of Medical Informatics, Volume 73, Issue 1, 2004.

[11]   L. sajn and M. Kukar, Image processing and machine learning for fully automated probabilistic evaluation of medical images, J. Computer Methods and Programs in Biomedicine, Volume 104, Issue 3, pp. 75-86, December 2011.

[12]   D. Krefting, M. Vossberg, A. Hoheisel and T. Tolxdorff, Simplified implementation of medical image processing algorithms into a grid using a workflow management system, J. Future Generation Computer Systems, Volume 26, Issue 4, pp. 681-684, April 2010.

[13]   S. E. Mahmoudi, A. Akhondi-Asl, R. Rahmani, S. Faghih-Roohi, V. Taimouri, A. Sabouri and H. Soltanian-Zadeh, Web-based interactive 2D/3D medical image processing and visualization software, J. Computer Methods and Programs in Biomedicine, Volume 98, Issue 2, pp. 172-182, 2010.

[14]   A. Martinez and J. J. Jiménez, Tracking by means of geodesic region models applied to multidimensional and complex medical images, J. Computer Vision and Image Understanding, Volume 115, Issue 8, pp. 1083-1098, 2011.

[15]   L. Wei, Y. Yang and R. M. Nishikawa, Micro calassification assisted by content-based image retrieval for breast cancer diagnosis, J. Pattern Recognition, Volume 42, Issue 6, pp. 1126-1132, 2009.

[16]   D.R. Chen, Y.L. Huang and S.H. Lin, Computer-aided diagnosis with textural features for breast lesions in sonograms, J. Computerized Medical Imaging and Graphics, Volume 35, Issue 3, pp. 220-226, 2011.

[17]   W.J. Kuo, R.F. Chang, C. C. Lee, W. K. Moon and D.R. Chen, Retrieval technique for the diagnosis of solid breast tumors on sonogram, J. Ultrasound in Medicine and Biology, Volume 28, Issue 7, pp. 903-909, 2002.

[18]   U. Bottigli and B. Golosio, Feature extraction from mammographic images using fast marching methods, J. Nuclear Instruments and Methods in Physics, 3rd International Workshop on Radiation Imaging Detectors, Volume 487, Issues 1-2, pp. 209-215, 2002.

[19]   H. Pourghassem and H. Ghassemian, Content-based image classification using a new hierarchical merging sheme, journal of Computarized Medical Imaging and Graphics, vol. 32, pp. 561 - 661, 2008.

[20]   J.Q Yan, Q.1 li, L. Zhi, D. Zhang, and Q.L Tang, Classification of hyperspectral medical tongue images for tongue diagnosis, journal of Computerized Medical Imaging and Graphics, vol. 31, pp. 672-678, 2007.

[21]   B.C. Desai, Md.M. Rahman and P. Battacharya, Medical image retrieval with probabilistic multiclass support vector machine classifiers and adaptative similarity fusion, journal of Computerized Medical Imaging and Graphics, vol. 32, pp. 95 - 108, March 2008.

[22]   L. Nanni, A. Lumini and S. Bahnam, Local binary patterns variants as texture descriptors for medical image analysis, journal of Artificial Intelligence in Medicine, vol. 49, pp. 117 - 125, 2010.

[23]   Steeve Young, HTK book, Version 3.4, December 2006.

[24]   R. Chellappa, C.L. Wilson, S. Sirohey, Human and machines recognition of faces: a survey, Proc, pp. 705-740, 1995.

[25]   A. Samal, P.A. Lyengar, Automatic recognition and analysis of human faces and facial expressions: a survey, Pattern Recognition, pp. 65-77, 1992.

[26]   X. Zhang and Y. Gao, Face recognition across pose: Areview, J. Pattern Recognition, volume 42, Issue 11, pp. 2876-2896, 2009.

[27]   A.F. Abate, M.Nappi, D.Riccio, G.Sabatino, 2D and 3D face recognition: a survey, PatternRecognition Lett, pp. 1885-1906, 2007.

[28]   S.Z.Li, A.K.Jain, Handbook of Face Recognition, Springer, NewYork, 2005.

[29]   H.Wechsler, Reliable FaceRecognition Methods: SystemDesign, H.Wechsler, Reliable Face Recognition Methods: System Design, Implementation and Evaluation, Springer, Berlin, 2006.

[30]   W.Zhao, R.Chellappa, FaceProcessing: Advanced Modelingand Methods, Academic Press, NewYork, 2005.

[31]   A.L. Yuille, P.W. Hallinan, D.S. Cohen, Feature extraction from faces using deformable templates, Int. J Comput, pp. 99-111, 1992.

[32]   X. Xie, R. Sudhakar, H. Zhuang, On improving eye feature extraction using deformable templates, Pattern Recognition, pp. 791-799, 1994.

[33]   K.M. Lam, H. Yan, Location and extracting the eye in human face images, Pattern Recognition, pp. 771-779, 1996.

[34]   H. Okada, J. Stevens, T. Maurer, H. Hong, E. Elagin, H. Neven, C. Malsburg, The Bochum/USC face recognition system, Face Recognition: From Theory to Applications, Springer, Berlin, pp. 186-205, 1998.

[35]   H.H.S. Ip, J.M.C. Ng, Human face recognition using Dempster-Shafer theory. Proceedings of IEEE International Conference on Image Processing, pp. 292-295, 1994.

[36]   L. Wiskott, J.M. Fellous, N. Kruger, C. Malsburg, Face recognition by elastic bunch graph matching, IEEE Trans. Pattern Anal. Mach. Intell, pp. 775-780, 1997.

[37]   L. Sirovich, M. Kirby, Low-dimensional procedure for the characterization of human faces, J. Opt. Soc. Am, pp. 519-524, 1987.

[38]   M. Turk, A. Pentland, Eigenfaces for recognition, J. Cognitive Neurosci 3, Volume 1, pp. 71-86, 1991.

[39]   W. Zhao, A. Krishnaswamy, R. Chellappa, D.L. Swets, J. Weng, Discriminant analysis of principal components for face recognition, Face Recognition: From Theory to Applications, Springer, Berlin , pp. 73-85, 1988.

[40]   A. O'Toole, H. Abdi, K. De!enbacher, D. Valentin, Lowdimensional representation of faces in higher dimensions of the face space, J. Opt. Soc. Am. A, pp. 405-411, 1993.

[41]   S. Lawrence, C.L.Giles, A.C.Tsoi, A.D.Back, Face recognition: aconvolutional neural-network approach,IEEETrans.NeuralNetwork8, pp. 98-113, 1997.

[42]   R.Brunelli, T.Poggio, Facerecognition: features versus templates, IEEETrans. Pattern Anal.Mach.Intell.15, Volume 10, pp. 1042-1052, 1993.

[43]   L. Wiskott, J.M. Fellous, N. Kruger, C. vonderMalsburg, Face recognition by elastic bunch graph matching, IEEETrans. PatternAnal. Mach. Intell. 19, Volume 7, pp. 775-779, 1997.

[44]   The IRMA project web site: http://www.irma-project.org/

[45]   ORL database: http://www.cl.cam.ac.uk/research/dtg/attarchive/facedatabase.html

www.ingramcontent.com/pod-product-compliance
Lightning Source LLC
LaVergne TN
LVHW042342060326
832902LV00006B/343